GROWING UP IS...

Coping with
adult problems
when you're
still a kid.

Margery A. Kranyik, Ed.D.

Illustrated by Karen Silverman

BETTERWAY PUBLICATIONS, INC.
Whitehall, Virginia

Published by Betterway Publications, Inc.
White Hall, VA 22987

Book design by Diane Nelson
Illustrations by Karen Silverman
Typography by Graphic Communications

Copyright © 1985 by Margery A. Kranyik

All rights reserved. No part of this book may be reproduced by any means, except by a reviewer who wishes to quote brief excerpts in connection with a review in a magazine or newspaper.

Library of Congress Cataloging in Publication Data

Kranyik, Margery A.
   Growing up is . . .

   Bibliography: p.
   Includes index.
   1. Socially handicapped children – United States –
Juvenile literature. 2. Problem families – United States –
Juvenile literature. I. Silverman, Karen. II. Title.
HV741.K68 1985   362.7   85-1206
ISBN 0-932620-34-5 (pbk.)

Printed in the United States of America

To
Robert D. Kranyik,
my cousin, my mentor and my friend;
with thanks for being a constant source
of inspiration and support.

PREFACE

To Adults Who Read Growing Up Is. . .

Growing up in an adult world is not an easy task for young people. Family structure has changed. Society has gone from a single type of family to *many* types of families, all of which are now socially acceptable. Many young people must now learn to live with divorce, single parents, and stepfamilies. Each of these situations has its own set of problems. Young people do not always understand what is happening to them and why. All they know is that they often feel unhappy and frightened.

Their family concerns often affect other aspects of their lives—their friendships and their schoolwork. They fall prey to peer pressure, often getting lost in competition, vandalism and even drugs. Problems with teachers result in poor grades, expulsion and sometimes dropping out.

Growing Up Is. . . was written to help young people address their problems and see the need for talking out their feelings with someone who cares. Ideally, the greatest progress would be to have more young people talking with their parents, treating their parents as they would want their parents to treat them. Unfortunately, this does not always happen. They need to be shown, however, how to find adults with whom they *can* share feelings. Often these people are teachers, guidance counselors, community youth group leaders, camp counselors and friends' parents. The important thing is having *someone* with whom a young person can talk — someone who can reassure them that they are not alone in what they feel.

It is important for parents to remember that young people often do not know how to speak to adults — especially their parents. They are afraid that grown-ups will not understand or care about what they are feeling. They may feel that parents have enough problems and do not need to be burdened with others. Often they assume that they are the only persons to experience such feelings, not realizing that other young people share the same concerns. They should, therefore, be encouraged to talk to a parent on a one-to-one basis whenever possible. Have lunch together, prepare a special snack, take a walk or create any situation that will reduce stress and encourage communication.

As a parent, you may have to ask your young person to assume some family responsibilities. It is important for them to understand *why*. You may ask them to help with chores when they would rather be out playing with their friends. The conflict between trying to be grown-up while still being a kid can produce stress in a young person. Watch for changes in their behavior — withdrawing from the family, showing aggression toward others, exhibiting defiant behavior or poor performance in school. Any of these problems may indicate a need for all of you to discuss any stressful family situations that have resulted in the need for the young person to assume the responsibilities. They may need only to be reassured that you still love them.

Growing Up Is... is not only for young people who are experiencing problems themselves. It is also for those who are sharing the growing-up process with their friends who may be in trouble. Young people need to develop compassion. They need to try and understand what others are feeling when they are in trouble or upset. Perhaps the best they will be able to do is to be good listeners. This is important.

Preface

We live in a world where people can hear but do not actually listen to what others are trying to share.

How to Use GROWING UP IS...

Use the entire book or individual chapters. Make the book available to any young person or group of young people. Lead a discussion. Find out how they all feel about what they read. Ask if any of the readers ever had experiences similar to those mentioned in the book. If you give the book to a young person whom you know is having a particular difficulty, preface it with some discussion. Express your concern about any feelings, moods or behavior changes you observe. Follow up with a personal discussion with the young person involved if he or she seems receptive.

Often there is comfort in numbers. Individuals may not wish to admit at first, even to someone whom they trust, that they have a problem. Discuss the book with a small group. If you are able to initiate discussion with one or two in the group, others may soon choose to share their opinions and feelings. Recommend the books at the end of the chapters for further reading. The books may be useful in either solving personal problems or researching oral or written report topics for school. You may wish to add some of the other related titles to your personal or school library.

The books at the end of this chapter can supplement *Growing Up Is*. . . Look for them at your local library or bookstore.

GROWING UP IS...

Books For Parents

DIVORCE

Grollman, Earl A. *Talking About Divorce,* Boston: Beacon Press, 1968.

Kantzler, Mel. *Creative Divorce,* New York: New American Library, Inc., 1975.

Rowlands, Peter. *Saturday Parent,* New York: Continuum Publishing Co., Inc., 1982.

Shickel, Richard. *Singled Out,* New York: The Viking Press, Inc., 1980.

Troyer, Warner. *Divorced Kids,* New York: Harcourt, Brace and Jovanovich, Inc., 1979.

SINGLE PARENTING

Atlas, Stephen L. *Single Parenting: A Practical Resource Guide,* Englewood Cliffs, New Jersey: Prentice-Hall, Inc., 1981.

Baruth, Leroy G. *A Single Parent's Survival Guide,* Dubuque, Iowa: Kendall/Hunt Publishing Co., 1979.

Capaldi, Frederic P. and McRae, Barbara. *Stepfamilies: A Cooperative Responsibility,* New York: Franklin Watts, Inc., 1979.

Klein, Carole. *The Single Parent Experience,* New York: Avon Books, 1973.

Weiss, Robert. *Going It Alone,* New York: Basic Books, Inc., 1979.

STEPPARENTING

Berman, Claire. *Making It As A Stepparent,* Garden City, New York: Doubleday and Co. Inc., 1980.

Logas, Jeanette and Roosevelt, Ruth. *Living In Step,* New York: McGraw-Hill Book Co., 1977.

Visher, Emily B. and Visher, John S. *Stepfamilies,* New York: Brunner/Mazel, Inc., 1979.

CHILD ABUSE

Dolan, Edward F. Jr. *Child Abuse,* New York: Franklin Watts, Inc., 1980.

Kempe, Ruth S., and Kempe, C. Henry. *Child Abuse,* Cambridge, Massachusetts: Harvard University Press, 1978.

CRIME

Cain, Arthur H., Dr. *Young People and Crime,* New York: The John Day Company, 1968.

ADOLESCENCE

Renzler, Carol Eisen. *Your Adolescent: An Owner's Manual,* New York: Atheneum Publishers, 1980.

Table of Contents

PREFACE   To Adults Who Read *Growing Up Is* 5

INTRODUCTION 15

CHAPTER 1: The Changing Family 19
CHAPTER 2: Your Working Family 29
CHAPTER 3: On Your Own at Home 39
CHAPTER 4: Coping With a Family Crisis 53
CHAPTER 5: Going to a Specialty Camp 69
CHAPTER 6: Failing at School Does Not Mean You
           Are a Failure 71
CHAPTER 7: Surviving Peer Pressure 79
CHAPTER 8: Conclusion 89

APPENDIX 1: What Would You Do? 91
APPENDIX 2: Organizations for Young People 93
INDEX 95

Acknowledgments

I wish to thank Linda Rappaport, friend and early childhood specialist, for her endless support for *Growing Up Is...* Her successful work with young people has been a constant source of inspiration to me as a teacher and as an author.

A special thank you goes to Alicia Rappaport, my young reader who reassured me about the things young people need to know.

INTRODUCTION

It is often difficult to live in a grown-up world when you are still a kid. Your parents and other adults around you expect you to accept responsibility and to act grown-up. You *want* to be grown-up at times, but at the same time, would like to be a kid. Growing up sometimes is a problem and hard to understand.

Many changes in family life have occurred in the last few years that have made young people need to take on more and more responsibilities around the home.

Those of you with both of your parents working may find that you have many chores to do around your home, both before and after school. Sometimes it is difficult to accept these responsibilities when you would rather be playing or watching television. Your parents are not at home most of the day and when they do get home, they are often very tired.

If you live with one parent, you may have to do many chores while your parent is working. There will be meals to prepare, younger brothers and sisters to look after and more time spent keeping your home clean. You may be spending a lot of time by yourself after school and may not get to see your friends as often as you would like. Some young people spend this time after school at home while others are enrolled in an afterschool program in the community, where they go every day and during school vacation.

There may be a time when your parents are out of work. When this happens, there isn't much money available for your family to spend. You will find yourself not being able to afford to do things, by yourself and with your family, that have been fun. It makes parents upset not to have a job. When they are upset, you will feel bad, too. It is difficult to understand what is going on. Sometimes your parents are ashamed and do not talk to you about the problems. Then you feel left out.

Your entire family structure can suddenly change. Your parents may get divorced and later get married again. This means you may have a stepmother or stepfather and perhaps some stepbrothers and sisters. Then you will have to share a home with new people. This is difficult when you are used to being an important person in your home. Now you will have to share a home and the people in it. You may even have to move to a new place.

Your friends may cause problems by asking you to do things you know are wrong. You will have to decide what to do. Even though you want to be just like your friends, their ideas may get you into serious trouble. This, too, is part of the confusing world of growing up.

New living conditions at home and relationships with your friends may cause problems at school. It is difficult to keep your mind on your studies when you are worried or angry about things at home. Sometimes you feel that there is nobody to talk to—that nobody will understand or care about your problems.

This book, *Growing Up Is. . . Coping with Adult Problems When You're Still a Kid* was written to give you some help with your concerns. It will help explain why some of these problems have occurred and where you can go for help if you need it. Nobody can understand or solve problems if they are kept bottled up inside. Everyone needs someone with whom they can talk, whether it is a parent, a teacher, another adult, or a friend.

Introduction

Points to Remember as You Read This Book
- Treat your parents the way you would like them to treat you.
- When you are troubled, angry, or upset, talk to your parents about what is bothering you.
- If you cannot talk to your parents, talk to another adult whom you trust.
- Other young people have the same kind of problems and concerns that you do.
- You may have to assume responsibilities for yourself and for your family, that you really do not wish to have.
- Parents and other adults may need your help in learning how to talk with young people.
- Although you may not be number one at everything you do, you can feel good about the things you *can* do.
- Be a good listener to other young people who are having problems.
- It is difficult to be a young person in a grown-up world.

There are other books listed at the end of some of the chapters. If you would like to read more about the topics discussed in *Growing Up Is...*, talk with your school librarian or the librarian in the young adult section of your library.

1.
The Changing Family

Everyone belongs to a family. Some families have a few people in them while others are quite large. Your immediate family includes the people with whom you live. Some of you may have your mom or dad and yourself in your family. Others of you may live with Mom, Dad, and brothers or sisters. No matter how many of you there are, you still belong to a family that is *your* family.

How Families Have Changed

Members of families have had to move far away from each other because jobs have been difficult to find and parents need to work. It is not unusual for you to have other members of your family living across the country rather than across the street.

Many families have had a divorce and the young people live with only one parent. If your mom and dad are divorced, you are probably living with one parent and traveling to visit the other. Others of you may have only one parent. Still others of you may have a mom or dad who has remarried someone with children of his or her own. This means your family will include a stepmother or stepfather and some stepbrothers or stepsisters.

All of these new family styles do have problems occasionally. The problems can be helped, however, if all take time to talk about the

GROWING UP IS...

The Changing Family

things that bother them. Let us look at three types of family situations. Perhaps one of them applies to you or to one of your friends.

Divorced Families. Some of you may have parents that are divorced. More and more young people today are living with either their mom or their dad. If your parents are divorced, you may find that you are not the only person in your class to be in this situation.

It has probably been difficult for you to adjust to this new family style. For a while, you may even have thought that the divorce was your fault. You may have tried hard to get your parents to live together again. This usually does not work because the problems that have occurred have been building up for a long time. When this happens, it is better for each parent to live separately. If your parents feel unhappy with each other and still live with you and your brothers and sisters, it may make all of you feel uncomfortable. Sometimes, parents will fight and this will make you feel hurt and frightened.

In some cases, young people never see one of their parents again. This is sad. Most of the time, however, either Mom or Dad will have visitation rights which means he or she can be with you on weekends, certain days of the week, and school vacations. This means you will have your own bed in your room at home and have a bed in another house or apartment to sleep in during your visits.

Sometimes you feel as though you are caught right in the middle of your parents' problems. It may not be easy for them to live apart. Each one may ask you questions about what the other is doing. One parent may try to buy you new clothes and toys each time you visit. All of this can be very confusing to you. Even though your parents don't love each other, and no longer live together, they still love you and are trying very hard to make sure that you will still love them.

The important thing to remember is that no matter *where* your parents live, they are still your mom and dad. They probably feel bad about the divorce and are concerned about how you feel and what you think. They may not know how to begin to ask you about your feelings.

Try to talk with each parent about how you feel. Let them know that you love them. They need to know that. You may feel angry at your parent who left your home. This is a natural way to feel. Other young people have felt the same way. Divorce *is* something you can talk about. It may even make you cry. Your parents will not know what you are thinking, however, unless you share your feelings with them. Telling each of your parents what is on your mind may help all of you understand what has happened. Talking things out may help everyone learn to live in the new family situation. The books listed at the end of this chapter will tell you more about divorce.

Single-Parent Families. Some of you may live with only one parent all the time—either because the other one has gone away or died, or because your mom has chosen not to marry. This means that the parent with whom you live has to try to be both a mom and a dad to you, which really cannot happen.

Your help and support is very important to your single parent. He or she is working hard to make sure that all of you have a place to live, enough food to eat, clothes to wear, and toys with which to play. Many jobs do not pay much money, making it even harder for your parent to pay all the bills. Your parent needs to know that he or she can count on you to keep the house clean, look after a brother or sister, help prepare a meal, and take good care of yourself.

Although your family may include only you and one parent, this is still *your* family and is just as important as families with many members. Take some time to talk with other young people who are from single-parent families. You will find that all of you have many of the same feelings and concerns. There are books listed at the end of this chapter that will tell you more about living in single-parent families.

Stepfamilies. There may come a time when your divorced mom or dad may decide to remarry. This could present a new set of problems for you. The new person in your family will be your

The Changing Family

stepparent—either a stepmother or stepfather.

It may be difficult for you to adjust to this new person in your home—especially if you have been a very important person in the life of your mom or dad. Now someone else has come along and you may feel left out and unneeded. This is a natural feeling. Your parent, however, may need a partner to love and share his or her life. Your mom or dad will *not* stop loving you or sharing with you. You will *still* be important.

Actually, your parent needs your support now more than ever. Your mom or dad may have some scary feelings about remarrying. Adults have just as hard a time talking about their feelings as kids do. They wonder if they are doing the right thing—both for themselves and for you. They are not sure about what to say and sometimes they do not say anything. When neither of you speaks about problems, the problems seem to grow; then you and your parent may grow apart.

This is a most important time to let your parent know how you feel. Ask your mom or dad for a special meeting time. Plan to go to lunch or have a special snack together. You may want to write down some of the things that are troubling you so you will not forget. Your parent will want to know how you feel and will be relieved to be able to share the feelings.

If you do not feel comfortable talking, write a note. Some people express their feelings better with written words. The important thing is communication—opening the doors for you and your parent to express your feelings together.

Your parent may want you to talk to the person who is going to be your stepparent. This is even harder to do because you do not know this person as well as you know your parent. Your new stepparent is also going to be worried about how you will feel in this new family.

Give your new stepparent a chance. Stepparents in real life are not like the wicked people in fairy tales! He or she is not trying to replace your parent who no longer lives with you. You both have one thing in common—you both love the parent with whom you are living. This mutual love can help to build the new family.

You may learn to love your new stepparent and feel guilty about your parent who lives away. It is o.k. to love both of them. You will always love your biological parent in a special way that nobody will ever change. As you grow up, you will learn to love lots of people in different ways.

If you have new stepbrothers or stepsisters living with you, there may be more talking and confusion in your home than you had before. Ask your family for some time and a place that is off limits to everyone but you. You will need time to be by yourself to read, study, play, listen to music, or think.

Even though you may open the doors of communication, things will not always run smoothly. There will still be problems to face and challenges to meet along the way. It could take a year or more for everyone to get used to each other. You will have to live with these problems as best you can. Set meeting dates, write notes, or keep a suggestion box for all of you to express your feelings. Living with stepparents can teach you to get along with other people. Look at it this way—you will have more adults to give you attention!

Remember to listen to your parents' feelings the way you would like them to listen to yours. You cannot gain the respect you want from them unless you return the same respect. If everyone thinks about the others' feelings with love and understanding, everything will work out.

The books at the end of this chapter will help you to understand more about stepfamilies.

Books For You To Read

THE CHANGING FAMILY

Gay, Kathlyn. *A Family Is For Living: The Changing Family in a Changing World,* New York: Delacorte Press, 1972.

Rofes, Eric E. *The Kids' Book of Divorce,* New York: Random House-Vintage, 1982.

Tax, Meredith. *Families,* Boston: Little-Brown Publishing Co., 1981.

DIVORCE

Boechman, Charles. *Surviving Your Parents' Divorce,* New York: Franklin Watts, Inc., 1979.

Booher, Dianna D. *Coping: When Your Family Falls Apart,* New York: Julian Messner, 1979.

Gardner, Richard A., M.D. *The Boys and Girls Book About Divorce,* New York: Bantam Books, Inc., 1971.

Glass, Stuart. *A Divorce Dictionary,* Boston: Little, Brown and Co. Inc., 1980.

Grollman, Earl A. *Talking About Divorce,* Boston: Beacon Press, 1975.

Hyde, Margaret O. *My Friend Has Four Parents,* New York: McGraw-Hill Books, Inc., 1981.

Jackson, Michael and Jackson, Jessica. *Your Father's Not Coming Home Anymore,* New York: Richard Marek Publishers, 1981.

LeShan, Eda. *What's Going To Happen to Me?* New York: Four Winds Press, 1978.

Richards, Arlene and Willis, Irene. *How To Get It Together When Your Parents Are Coming Apart,* New York: Bantam Books, Inc., 1977.

Rofes, Eric E., Ed. *The Kids' Book Of Divorce: By, For And About Kids,* Lexington, Massachusetts: Lewis Publishing Company, 1981.

Spilke, Francine Susan. *What About Me? Understanding Your Parents' Divorce,* New York: Crown Publishers, Inc., 1979.

White, Ann S. *Divorce,* New York: Franklin Watts, Inc., 1979.

SINGLE PARENTS

Gardner, Richard A., M.D. *The Boys' And Girls' Book About One Parent Families,* New York: G.P. Putnam's Sons, Inc., 1978.

Gilbert, Sara. *How To Live With A Single Parent,* New York: Lothrop, Lee and Shepard Books, 1982.

Schwarts, Sheila. *Like Mother, Like Me,* New York: Pantheon Books, 1978.

STEPFAMILIES

Berman, Claire. *What Am I Doing In A Stepfamily?* Secaucus, New Jersey: Lyle Stuart, 1982.

Bradley, Buff. *Where Do I Belong? The Kids' Guide To Stepfamilies,* Reading, Massachusetts: Addison-Wesley Publishing Co., 1982.

Burt, Roger and Burt, Mala. *What's Special About Our Stepfamily,* Garden City, New York: Doubleday and Company, 1983.

Craven, Linda. *Stepfamilies: New Patterns In Harmony,* New York: Simon and Schuster, Inc., 1982.

Einstein, Elizabeth. *The Stepfamily: Living, Loving and Learning,* New York: The Macmillan Co. Inc., 1982.

Sobol, Harriet Langsam. *My Other Mother, My Other Father,* New York: Macmillan Co. Inc., 1979.

2.

Your Working Family

In many families today, all of the adults have to go to work in order to pay the household bills and buy food. It costs a lot of money to pay the rent and the gas, electric, and phone bills, and to buy gasoline for the car and fuel for the home. The cost of food at the supermarket increases each week. With these costs increasing, parents have to work hard and often for long hours to have enough money to look after your family. Some parents do not have money left over from paying the bills to have fun, such as going to the movies or out to a restaurant to eat. You may not be able to have the birthday or holiday gifts that you want.

Parents feel bad when they do not have the money to do special things. They want their children to have nice clothes and toys. They would like to take vacations, but sometimes that just cannot happen. All of these things cost money and parents cannot always afford them.

Some parents work because they have spent much time and money preparing for a career, and do not wish to give it up. Years ago, mothers stayed at home keeping house and looking after their children. Today, however, many mothers are doctors, lawyers, accountants, and teachers who wish to keep practicing what they learned in college.

GROWING UP IS...

Your Working Family

When all the adults in the family are working, that often means that you will have special chores to do daily while your parents are at work and you are at home. You may have to make breakfast and lunch for yourself and your brothers and sisters. You may have to help with the laundry, get dinner started or do some cleaning around your house or apartment. You may even have to babysit for younger brothers or sisters when you would rather be playing with your friends. Having to do all these chores may make you feel angry at your parents. You may feel that they really don't care about you and just use you to do work around the house. They really *do* care, however, and often moms feel guilty because they have to go to work and leave you with household jobs to do.

Having to do chores around your home can make you feel confused. One minute you feel like a grown-up, doing things that grown-ups have to do. The next minute you feel like a little kid who really doesn't want to do all that work. Parents feel confused, too. Sometimes they treat you like a grown-up. They count on you to get chores done. At another time they don't want you to bother them because they are too tired from work or too busy with work around the house.

It is normal to feel angry and confused at those times. When that happens, ask your parents if all of you can set up a meeting—maybe on the weekend when everyone has some free time. Tell your parents how you feel. Ask them to tell you how *they* feel. Ask questions if you really do not understand why they have to go to work. Sometimes parents forget that you have feelings. Remind them.

Parents are often tired and cranky when they come home at the end of the work day. When you want to tell them something important that happened to you during the day, they may be too tired or too busy making dinner to listen. This can make you feel like they don't care—but they really do. Sometimes grown-ups do not like their job—as you do not always like school. Because jobs are difficult to find, your parents have to remain at their work, like it or not. This can make them grumpy, too.

Give your parents time to get settled when they come home at the end of a busy day. Ask them about *their* day. Did something nice happen? You may not understand all of what they are saying — just like they do not always understand some of the things you do at school. Be a good listener to your parents — the way you would like them to listen to you.

Pay attention when someone asks you to lower the sound on the television, radio or tape deck. Sometimes loud noises can make tired people more cranky.

There may be times when it is difficult to keep from fighting with your brothers and sisters. Dinner time is a time when *everyone* is tired and hungry. Even you have had a busy day. Tempers can be short. Try to work problems out among you without involving Mom or Dad.

Everyone in the family has to give and take a little bit. Give up some television time and play time to talk with your parents. Perhaps you and your mom and dad can talk for a few minutes before you go to bed. Instead of a bedtime story like you had when you were younger — you can ask for bedtime talk!

You may have a parent who has to go to work nights. Since night jobs often pay more money than day jobs, your parent may need to work nights. This means you won't see your night-job parent very often. When he or she is coming home after work in the morning, you will be off to school. When you get home from school in the late afternoon, your parent will be going off to work.

Sometimes, your parent's night job can affect your life. People who work nights have to sleep during the day. You may have to play quietly or away from your home so your parent can get enough sleep. This can make you feel sad because you do not get to spend enough time with your parent. You may feel angry because your sleeping parent interrupts your play.

You may even be grouchy at school. Sean, a little boy in second grade, suddenly became tired and inattentive at school. When the teacher questioned his mother, she found out that Sean's father had gone to work nights for the first time. He and Sean used to read bedtime stories together every night. Sean missed his dad's special time with him and couldn't fall asleep at night. This is why he was tired at school. Parents' work schedules can have an important effect on how a family lives each day.

Set up a special date with your parents to talk about what you are feeling. Since you cannot have all of their time, make your time special—for you and them. Plan a lunch, a movie, a walk on the beach or in the park. Mark it on the calendar. Your parents need to know that you want to be with them. Treat your parents the same way you would like them to treat you.

Earning Your Own Money

Even you can be a part of a working family. Your parents may give you an allowance each week. The money you receive may be in return for the chores that you are asked to do around the house each day. This exchange is preparing you for the same type of responsibility that grown-ups have when they work—receiving money for a job that is done. In some cases, your parents may give you your allowance with no strings attached, meaning it is yours to spend in any way that you would like. Others of you may be asked to put a portion of your allowance away for savings or for church. In any case, you will have to make the money last for at least a week.

For some of you this will be easy once you decide how you wish to spend your money. For others, you may find yourself having spent all your money by the middle of the week. This creates a big problem if you have a movie that you wish to see on Friday night and no money left. Your parents may choose not to give you any more money or to advance you money from next week's allowance. Grown-ups cannot ask the boss for more money if they spend it all before the next pay day. They have to wait until their next pay check and *you* should have to wait until your next allowance. After you have been disappointed a few times, you will learn to budget and save some of your money for unexpected things that may occur at the end of each week. Shown below is a sample budget plan to help you spend wisely.

Your Sample Budget

Grown-ups often make a budget – a list of their expenses – so they will know how to spend their money wisely. Try making your own budget to see where and how you are spending your money. If you plan ahead, you will not run out of money at the end of the week. Then you will not risk being able to do something special with your friends. If you can tell your parents how you spend your money, you may be able to negotiate a raise in your allowance.

List all of the things on which you spend your money *and* the cost, such as:

Movies, roller skating, ice skating	$2.00
Popcorn, drinks, candy	$1.25
Video games	$1.00
Snack at drug store	$ .50
Total	$4.75

If you start with a $5.00 allowance, you will have $.25 left at the end of the week. If you have money left over, you should have a jar or a bank where you can save what is left for something special. Some weeks you may *not* have anything left over.

Remember to *plan ahead.* If you go to the movies at the end of the week, you will have to set that money aside so you will not spend it before the weekend.

You may be able to work out a deal with your parents to earn extra money. Find out if there are other chores that you can do for more money. There may be some closets that need to be cleaned or a garage floor that should be swept.

Your neighborhood may offer opportunities for earning extra money. Elderly neighbors may need someone to help move furniture, clean a house or apartment, mow a lawn, or rake a yard. You could do these odd jobs occasionally after school or on a Saturday and have a few more dollars to spend on a special treat.

There are books listed at the end of the chapter that will give you some ideas about how to earn your own money. Look for them at your school or neighborhood library.

Books For You To Read

EARNING YOUR OWN MONEY

Amazing Life Games Company and Friends. *Good Cents: Every Kid's Guide To Making Money,* New York: Houghton Mifflin Company, 1974.

Byers, Patricia and Preston, Julia. *Kids' Money Book,* Cockeysville, Maryland: Liberty Publishing Co. Inc., 1983.

Lewis, Shari. *How Kids Can Really Make Money,* New York: Holt, Rinehart and Winston, 1979.

Sattler, Helen Roney. *Dollars From Dandelions: 101 Ways To Earn Money,* New York: Lothrop, Lee and Shepard Company, 1979.

Young, Jim and Young, Jean. *The Kid's Money Making Book,* Garden City, New York: Doubleday and Company, 1976.

3.

On Your Own at Home

When all the adults in your home are at work, you may have some time after school when you are home all alone. It can make you feel grown-up to be in the house or apartment all by yourself, but you do need to be careful and observe some basic rules.

Your Key. If you have a key to get into your home, keep it well hidden. Wear it on a chain around your neck under your clothes or keep it in a deep pocket. You should not let others know that you will be alone at home. If you lose your key, tell your teacher and your parents right away. Arrange for a neighbor to have an extra key.

House Rules. Your parents will tell you what they expect from you after school. Perhaps you could make up the rules together. House rules are important to follow. Your parents make them up for safety reasons. You will find a checklist of some house rules you might need at the end of this chapter.

Walk home from school the same way every day so that neighbors and people who live along the way will see you. Walk with your friends whenever possible.

Be at home before it gets dark. Wearing a watch will help you know what time it is. If you don't have your own watch, ask your parents for one for your birthday or a holiday, or save your money to buy one. There are many people on their way home at the end of the day who may not see young people walking at the side of the road. Ask your parents to put one of the lights in your home on an automatic timer in case you do get home after dark.

Play with your friends outdoors, or in their home only if an adult is in the house. Never bring your friends into your home when your parents are at work.

You may have a friend visiting you who will do things you know your parents would not like. If this should happen, ask your friend to stop or leave. If this does not work, call your parent or a neighbor right away.

If you go to visit a friend, be sure to tell your brothers or sisters or your parents where you will be.

If your parents have asked you *not* to leave the house, pay attention to their wishes. Don't go off to the store even for a quick trip. Your parents may need to call to give you a message and will worry if you are not there.

Be sure to keep all the doors locked after you get home. Have handy the name and telephone number of where your parents work. If they ask you to call them every day when you get home from school, be sure you do it. If you forget, your parents will worry and not do their jobs well.

Parents are concerned for your safety because, occasionally, children get kidnapped. People take children belonging to other people because they do not have any of their own or because they want to do things that are not nice for kids. Television programs have been produced about the kidnapping of children and young people. Ask your parents or a favorite adult to tell you about the dangers of kidnapping.

Do not phone your working parent with questions, problems, or complaints about your brothers and sisters that can wait until later. Your mom or dad has work that must be done by the end of the day—just like you do at school—and they should not be interrupted at their job except in case of emergency.

Have the telephone number of a neighbor or relative as a back-up person in case your parents cannot be reached. Your telephone is your link to the rest of the world. Use it for brief calls and in case of emergency. It may be fun to talk to your friends after school *and* talking may keep you from feeling scared. It is not a good idea, however, to tie up the telephone in case your parents need to reach you with an important message.

Keep a pen or pencil and pad near the telephone. If you should receive a call from a relative or a friend of your family, be sure to take the message and phone number. Sometimes parents get annoyed if you forget to tell them about an important call.

If you should miss the school bus, call your parent from school right away. Your working parent will worry if you do not call at the time you are expected to be at home.

Preparing Snacks and Meals. You and your parent should decide what foods you may eat after school and how they should be prepared. Stoves and microwave ovens can be dangerous if they are not used properly. Use them only if you have permission. Make sure you know how to operate the appliance and what to do or whom to call if something goes wrong.

Eat snacks that do not need much cooking. Cold snacks can be tasty and nutritious. It is nice to prepare a surprise treat for your parents, but it is safer to wait and cook meals with adult supervision. There is a list of simple no-cook snacks at the end of the chapter.

Clean up after yourself and your brothers and sisters. Wipe up any spills on the floor so nobody will slip and fall. Parents do not like to find dirty dishes in the sink and crumbs on the floor and table when they come home from work.

If you run out of a certain food, soap powder, or toilet tissue, write it on a shopping list. Parents really blow a fuse if they find they are out of something when they are in a rush to go someplace.

You may be asked to start dinner by defrosting food or turning on the oven. This is a big help to your parent who may be tired and ready for dinner at the end of the day. If you forget, dinner will be later or your family will have to spend money that they do not have, eating out in a restaurant.

Caring for Younger Children. There are times when caring for younger brothers and sisters can be a real pain. They *are* a part of your family, however, and just as important to your mom and dad as you are. You need to respect their rights the same way you would like them to respect yours. You may be asked to prepare their breakfast and school lunch each morning, meet them after school, and see that they have a snack when they arrive home. If your parents have given *you* the responsibility for helping the younger ones, it is because they trust *you* to do the job. The younger person may need and depend on your help. If you play together, play away from furniture that might break if all of you become too playful. Be careful near stairs and rugs that can be slippery. If you each have your own friends, tell each other where you are going to play.

If your brothers and sisters do not pay attention to the house rules, keep a list of what is going wrong. Be careful, however, that you are not being too bossy with the younger ones. Call a meeting with your parents *and* the other children. Quietly tell them what is bothering you. Look at your list for help. Having a list of exactly what went wrong is a more grown-up way of handling the problem than saying "He or she is being a creep or a pain." Your list will help your folks understand what is happening when they are not there. You and your parents may need to make a chart that lists everyone's jobs for each day of the week.

If You Are Sick. There may be times when you are home all day because you are too sick to go to school. Make sure that a back-up neighbor knows that you are home. Read or play quiet games. Stay in bed or rest on the sofa. Eat only what your mom or dad tells you to

On Your Own at Home

eat. Do not take any medicine unless you are told exactly *what* to take and *when* to take it. If you feel lonesome, keep your radio or television on. If you should feel much sicker during the day, call your parent or your neighbor.

At Home Before School. Your parents may have to leave for work in the morning before you have to leave for school each day. You will need to see that you have all your equipment that you need for school ready to take with you. You will also need to see that your home is locked up and secure for the day. This is an important job for you because you will not be able to call someone if you forget to lock a door or turn a light off. At the end of this chapter is a sample list of things to do before you leave for school. Make your own list and post it near the door so you will have a reminder each day.

What To Do in an Emergency

Make sure you have near the phone the number of the police department, fire department, your parent at work, a neighbor, and the person in charge of maintenance if you live in an apartment. A sample list of telephone numbers is included at the end of this chapter. If you have more than one telephone in your home, keep a list near each one.

In Case of Fire. Get everyone out of the house right away. Do not try to put out the fire yourself. This is the firefighters' job. Do not stop to get your favorite toy. Wasted seconds could cost you your life. Yell "FIRE" as loud as you can so people around your neighborhood will know there is trouble. Run to your nearest neighbor and call the fire department. If you have a fire in your apartment, do *not* use the elevator. Leave the building by the stairway.

Ask your family to help you plan a family escape route in case of fire. It is important for everyone in your family to know the different ways to escape from your home in case one way is blocked by fire. Have your own fire drills to practice getting out in case of fire.

GROWING UP IS...

Check for fire hazards that may exist in your home. Your family may be too busy to notice.

Keep matches and lighters out of reach of the younger children.

Keep paper away from the stove.

Check for electrical cords that are worn out.

Keep barbecue lighter and gasoline away from younger children.

If you should smell gas, leave the house right away. Do not use the phone. Go to a neighbor's house to call the fire department.

Keep a pan lid and a box of baking soda near the stove when you cook. If a pan of food or grease catches fire, cover it quickly with the lid and baking soda. Do *not* throw water on the stove.

Do not light your fireplace, woodburning stove or candles without supervision. Make sure you have flashlights in case of a power failure. Check the batteries in your flashlight occasionally, to see if they are still working.

If your clothing should catch on fire, drop to the floor and roll around. This will smother the flames. Yell for help.

Stranger on the Phone. If a stranger calls on the telephone while you are at home alone, tell them that your parent is busy right now and will call them back. *Never* say that nobody is home. Practice with your parents or with a friend what you would say to a stranger on the telephone.

Stranger at the Door. Do not open the door to anyone who comes to your home when you are there alone. Talk to them through the closed door. Ask them who they are. Tell them that your parent is busy and cannot come to the door. Even if the person tells you they need to use the telephone because their car broke down, tell them your mother is on the phone and they should go to a neighbor's house. Do not feel embarrassed to do this. If the person will not go away, go straight to the telephone and call the police.

Stranger in the Hallway. If you live in an apartment and meet someone in the hall who tries to follow you, run down the stairs.

Knock on a neighbor's door. Always remember to yell as loudly as you can so you will attract people's attention and get help.

Stranger Offers You a Ride. If a stranger offers you a ride from school or from where you are playing, do not go, even if the person offers you candy or money. Run as fast as you can to where there are people and tell them what has happened. Be *sure* to tell your parents and teachers any time that something scares you or makes you feel strange.

Even if someone calls you by name and tells you that your parents sent him or her to pick you up, do not go. Run to a nearby house.

Stranger who claims to be an old friend or relative of your parents. If someone tells you he is an old friend of your parents or that he is a distant relative who knew you "when you were still in diapers," do not go with him—no matter how nice and honest he seems to be. If he is the person he says he is, he will be in touch with your parents.

Power Outage. If the electricity in your home goes off, first look to see if the power is out all over your neighborhood or just in your home or building. Call your parent or contact person. They may ask you to call the electric company if the outage is in your neighborhood.

If the lights are out *only* in your home, light your flashlight and wait for your parent or contact person. *Never, never* light a candle to help you see. Candles can cause a fire.

Leaking Pipes. Have your parents show you where the shut-off valves are located in your home. If you come home and find a flood in your kitchen or bathroom, turn off the water at the main valve. Call your parent or contact person quickly. Water can cause expensive damage to floors and carpets in your home.

In Case of Accident. If you or your brother or sister gets hurt, call your parent or your back-up neighbor. If nobody is available, call an ambulance or rescue squad. Do not try to be your own doctor. In case of loss of blood or broken bones, time is very important. Try to

prevent accidents before they happen:
- Avoid climbing to high places where you might fall.
- Make sure all knives, medicines, sharp tools and household cleaners are out of the reach of younger children.
- Avoid rough-house playing indoors.

Be sure and tell your parents if anything goes wrong while they are away — even if it is your fault. They will want to know if you had even a *slight* injury or if an appliance is not working properly.

If you come home after school and something does not look right — a light is out, a door open or a strange car is parked nearby — go to a neighbor's home. Do not be afraid to ask for help. Sometimes our instincts seem to tell us that something is not right. It is a good idea to pay attention to our instincts, though we may turn out to be wrong.

Be good to yourself if you are home alone after school. Put that time to good use and add to your talents. Instead of watching television until your folks come home, do your homework, read a book or magazine or learn a new skill such as painting, needlework or woodworking. If you feel better having sounds in the house, turn on the radio for background talk and music.

You may find that being on your own after school every day makes you feel frightened and uncomfortable. If this is true, call a meeting with your parents. Tell them how you feel. There are places you might be able to go after school that are open for young people just like you. The YMCA, YWCA, Boys and Girls Clubs, Community Schools and some public school systems have after-school programs and vacation camps. Get some of your friends to look at some programs with you. It isn't like going to school again. These after-school programs offer arts and crafts, sports, and other recreational activities each day. Most of these programs do not cost a lot of money and may make you and your family a little more comfortable each day.

Dial-A-Pal. Many communities look for ways to help young people cope with things that may be bothering them when they are on their own. One community in Pennsylvania has a special "help line" that kids can call for help and advice. They try to answer questions such as "My cat just ran out the front door and I'm not supposed to leave the house. What shall I do? The people on the help line will also talk to kids who call in because they are afraid of thunder and lightning storms when they are home alone. It is good to have somebody to talk to in case your parent and contact person are not available.

Find out if your community has such a service. If not, talk to a teacher or youth group leader about the possibility of starting a help line. There are adults who may have time for such a project.

HOUSE RULES CHECKLIST

This list is only a suggestion. Make up your own list. Talk to your family about adding things that are important for you.

> Call Mom or Dad at work.
> Lock all doors.
> Meet brothers/sisters at the bus.
> Make snacks.
> Do homework.
> Do household chores.
> Start dinner.

BEFORE-YOU-LEAVE LIST

> Be sure you have your key.
> Turn off the lights.
> Take everything you need for school.
> Put pets in their proper place (either in or out).
> Make sure the stove and water are turned off.
> Lock all doors; Close and lock the windows in case of rain.

NO-COOK SNACKS

These snacks are easy to prepare and require no cooking. Look in your town and school library for cook books that will help you to make basic, nutritious, after-school munchies.

Vegetables

Carrots   Tomatoes
Celery   Squash

Add some lettuce and make a salad.

Fruit

Bananas   Apples
Grapes   Pears
Oranges

Try a delicious fruit salad.

Nuts   Crackers
Raisins   Sunflower seeds
Dried fruit   Applesauce
Yogurt   Granola bar
Cheese   Cereal

Combine some of these foods to make a special treat.

Pita bread filled with vegetables and cheese
Peanut butter and jelly
Apples and cheese
Cheese and crackers
Celery stuffed with cream cheese or peanut butter
Cheese spread on bread or crackers

On Your Own at Home

IMPORTANT PHONE NUMBERS

Your name _____
Your telephone number _____
Your address _____Apartment Number _____

MOM AT WORK _____
DAD AT WORK _____
BROTHER/SISTER AT SCHOOL _____
CONTACT PERSON _____
NEIGHBOR _____
RELATIVE _____
FIRE _____
POLICE _____
DOCTOR _____
RESCUE SQUAD _____
POISON CONTROL _____
VETERINARIAN _____
MAINTENANCE _____
(if you live in an apartment)

GROWING UP IS...

Books For You To Read

GROWING UP

Burns, Marilyn. *I Am Not A Short Adult! Getting Good At Being A Kid,* Boston: Little, Brown and Company, 1977.

Chapman, Arthur H. *Parents Talking, Kids Talking,* New York: G.P. Putnam's Sons, 1979.

Gilbert, Sara. *By Yourself,* New York: Lothrop, Lee and Shepard Books, 1983.

Hautzig, Esther. *Life With Working Parents: Practical Hints For Everyday Situations,* New York: Macmillan Publishing Co. Inc., 1976.

Kyte, Kathy S. *In Charge: A Complete Handbook For Kids With Working Parents,* New York: Alfred A. Knopf Inc., 1983.

Long, Thomas and Long, Lynette. *The Handbook For Latchkey Children And Their Parents,* New York: Arbor House Publishing Co., 1983.

Marsh, Carole. *Kids' Book of Smarts,* Tryon, North Carolina. Gallopade Publishing Group, 1983.

4.

Coping With Family Problems

Family life does not always go smoothly. Events may occur that change the way your family lives and acts. Sometimes the events are unpleasant things that make young people feel frightened, angry, and sad. Everyone's family has a problem occasionally. People go through life finding ways to solve their problems and still continue with their lives.

Your family may develop serious problems someday. These problems may affect you. You may have trouble understanding what is happening — especially if your family is afraid or ashamed to talk to you. Parents do not always know how to talk to young people. They are afraid they will say the wrong thing and therefore do not say anything at all. They may try to protect you from unhappiness and fear by pretending that everything is o.k. They forget that you are a smart person and that you will be able to tell when the people close to you are unhappy or in trouble.

Family secrets are not good to keep if they make you feel bad and do poorly in school. It is important to talk with someone even though your parents may ask you not to tell anyone.

Teachers, counselors and youth leaders know where you can go for help. You may want to read more about how other people solve family problems. There are books listed at the end of this chapter that will tell you more about living with a family crisis.

Let us look at some of the problems that might occur with families. They may not happen to you *but* may happen to a friend. It is a good idea for you to know about these problems so that you can be a good listener.

Unemployment. For the past few years we have been living in a world where jobs have been difficult to find and difficult to keep for many people. Perhaps some of you have had parents who have lost their jobs and have been out of work. This means that your family has had little or no money to buy food and pay the household bills. If your parent is out of work for a long time, all the money that he or she has saved in the bank has to be spent to take care of the family.

When parents do not have any money to support their family, they can apply to the state government to a program called welfare. If you have welfare help, the state will give your family a small amount of money each month to take care of buying food and paying bills. Sometimes this money is barely enough to take care of your family needs.

Most parents do not like to be on welfare. They would much rather be working for their money than to have it given to them when it has not been earned.

If your parents do not work for a long time, they may become unhappy and angry. They need to feel that they are able to support their family. When they cannot, they feel useless and like a failure.

If parents have not been able to find work, it may begin to affect the way they act at home. A parent who once was happy and laughed a lot may suddenly become quiet and unhappy. Parents may yell at you and even hit you when you do not deserve it. Some parents become involved with alcohol and drugs because it helps them to take their minds off the fact that they are not working. These are not answers to the problem because parents end up hurting themselves even more and they make you feel bad.

If your parent is unemployed, ask what you can do to help. Earn some of your own money by baby-sitting or getting a paper route. You may have to give up some of the lessons you are taking to cut down on expenses. Learn to make your own gifts for friends instead of buying them.

Life with a Parent Who Drinks. You may be living with a parent who drinks too much alcohol. Some adults can drink alcohol at a party or before dinner with no effects. Other adults, however, cannot stop drinking once they start. Their problem is called *alcoholism,* which is an illness.

Having an alcoholic parent can be embarrassing to a young person. If your mom or dad drinks too much, it may mean that they talk funny, walk unsteadily, fall asleep during the day, and dress untidily. They may yell and fight a lot. You probably will not want to bring your friends to your home because you do not know how your parent will act when he or she is drunk.

People who become alcoholics may have started drinking because the effects of alcohol make them happy and made them forget their problems for a while. An alcoholic usually cannot stop drinking without medical and psychological help. They may want to stop, but their bodies have become what we call *addicted.* They cannot stop drinking until they fall asleep. Even though you may want your parent to stop drinking, he or she really cannot stop. Adults must make the decision to stop drinking and seek help all by themselves.

If the noise and confusion at home caused by a drinking parent bothers you, you need to go where you can be by yourself. Take some time to fix up your room just the way you would like it to be. Make sure you have a comfortable place to read and write. A radio or tape player will help drown out unpleasant sounds from other parts of your home. Your room can be your "den" where you can do things that are important to you.

Get involved with other young people. Visit them often after school

GROWING UP IS...

and on weekends. If you have relatives—aunts, uncles and grandparents—nearby, get into the habit of visiting with them. They are part of your family—people who can provide you with love and attention.

Join some organizations that meet after school and on weekends. The "Y," scouts, 4-H club and the library all have programs for young people. If you like sports, there may be teams for young people that play when school is not in session.

Everyone needs a friend with whom they can talk. When someone in your family drinks, you need people around whom you can trust. Although your parents may have told you never to talk about what goes on at home, you cannot keep unpleasant things bottled up inside you. You need to talk with somebody. Talking gives you comfort and makes you feel better.

Sometimes a teacher or adjustment counselor at school can help you. Perhaps your priest, rabbi or pastor can assist your parent in getting help.

Talk with your older brothers or sisters or other relatives. They will have feelings about the family that they can share with you if they know you are upset. Talk with someone at school or in your community whom you trust. Talking with special friends about your parent's drinking problem can make you feel better about yourself.

The important thing about living with alcoholic parents is that their problem is not your fault. No matter how hard you try to do something to make them stop drinking, nothing will work unless they want to stop.

Other young people are in the same situation that you are. Many have sought help through an organization called Alateen. Alateen was started for people just like you to meet together and talk about what it is like to live with a parent who drinks. Look in your telephone book under AA or Al-Anon. Call the number and ask the person who answers if there is an Alateen program near your home.

Coping with a Family Crisis

If there is no Alateen program in your community, write a letter to:
  Teen Secretary
  Al-Anon Family Group Headquarters
  Box 182
  Madison Square Station
  New York, New York 10010

They will send you information in an unmarked envelope so nobody in your family will know if you do not wish to tell them.

The books listed at the end of this chapter will give you more information about how to live with a parent who drinks. Look for them in your library.

Drug Abuse. You have probably heard adults talk about the concerns they have for young people who use marijuana, cocaine, heroin and other drugs. Young people are not the only ones who become addicted to drugs. It can also happen to adults. They may try doing drugs to see what it is like—the same way that young people start. After a while, they cannot stop—the same way it is when they drink too much alcohol.

When people take too many drugs, they may behave in the same manner as people who drink too much. They may act silly and be noisy. Other times they may be depressed and unhappy. This can affect the life of a young person living in that home.

Drugs are expensive and often people do not have enough money to pay for their drug habit. When this happens, they steal money or items that they sell for money. When they are caught, they are arrested by the police.

People who use drugs will need medical help in order to stop. They will have to be enrolled in a special drug program in a hospital, the same as alcoholics.

It is not a pleasant feeling to have someone you love begin to behave strangely or end up in jail. Since you will not be able to do anything about it, however, you must continue doing what is best for yourself. Talk with a friend or counselor about your feelings. Remember that it helps to talk rather than to keep what you are thinking and feeling bottled up inside of you.

Child Abuse. When parents are unhappy about their lives, they do not always have patience with the people around them. You may find that suddenly your parent becomes angry and yells at you often. There may be times when he or she hits you. You must not allow this to happen. You could be hurt.

If your parent yells a lot or hits you, you *must* tell someone about it. Your parent needs help right away. Hitting people is not a way of showing love. Parents may hug and kiss you after they hit you. They may tell you that they are sorry and will never do it again. It *will* happen again and next time it could be worse.

You may feel sorry for your parent and may not want to tell anyone that you are being hurt. This is a normal way to feel. You *must*, however, tell someone you have been hit. No one should use you as a punching bag. Your body belongs to you and *nobody* should hit you or touch any private parts of your body.

Even though he or she hits you, your parent still loves you. This is hard to understand. It means your parent cannot control how he or she reacts to problems. Tell your teacher, a relative or a friend, even though you love your parent very much. They will get help for you right away.

The person who will help is called a social worker. The social worker will talk to both you and your parent. Answer any questions honestly. Remember, your parent needs help. You are not being mean by telling the truth. Nobody will take you away from your family unless it is dangerous for you to live in your home. The social worker will help your parent learn how to solve or live with the problems. Their job is to do everything possible to keep a family together.

It may take some time for you and your family to work out the problems. You may have to talk to a lot of people—even the police. The important thing to remember is that *you* may have to be the one to look for help for yourself and for your parent.

Death in the Family. Death is a subject no one likes to talk about. You may know someone in your class whose mom or dad has died. You might even lose someone who is close to you—your mom, dad, grandparents or friend. If this should happen, you will experience many different kinds of feelings.

The death of someone close affects everyone differently. It is, however, something that all people experience in their lifetime. You may have felt sadness when your dog or cat died. You will feel a greater sadness when some person close to you dies. You may feel hurt and abandoned because the person has gone and left you behind. Tom expressed anger about his father's death when he said, "Why did he have to die? He didn't even say good-bye."

Sometimes death happens so quickly that people cannot prepare for it. Even when you know that someone is going to die, you are never really ready when it happens.

You will miss that special person very much. It is difficult to accept the fact that someone you love is never coming back again. Karen and her grandmother played cards together almost every day. After her grandmother died, Karen didn't play cards for a long time. Cards made her sad because they reminded her of her grandmother and the good times they had together.

If someone close to you dies, remember that it is o.k. to cry. Others in your family will cry too. Sometimes you may not be able to cry. You may feel numb because of the shock of losing someone special. Your feelings will come out later when things quiet down.

Talk about what you are feeling with another member of your family, a teacher, or a friend. Remember the good times you shared with that person. Those memories will always live with you.

Ask someone in your family if you can have a book, scarf or other momento that belonged to the person who has died. This will help you to remember that although the person is no longer there, he or she will still live on in your heart.

People may avoid talking to you about the death because they are uncomfortable and do not know what to say. They are afraid they will make you feel worse. Tell them it is o.k. to mention the person who has died. Talk about the good memories you have.

There is a list of books about death at the end of this chapter. Look for them in your school or local library.

Living with an Ill Parent or Sibling. If someone in your family is seriously ill, you may find yourself spending time alone or with friends while the sick person is getting all your parents' attention. They may be visiting the hospital for many hours each day. If the ill person is at home, they may be having meals in bed. Other members of the family may spend much time talking to the person or just sitting with them.

You may feel *jealous*—a feeling you have when you think your parent likes someone else better than you or is spending more time with someone than they are with you. You will feel hurt and often lonesome. Sometimes you may feel insecure about what is happening to the person, especially if your parents do not tell you anything.

Parents may not talk to you about what is going on because they are afraid that you will worry. They forget that you will worry about things you *do not* know and *do not* understand. You will need to sit down and tell your parent how you feel. Ask questions about the person who is ill. Ask your parents how you can be of help. You may be able to talk to the ill person or read to them. Perhaps the most help you can offer is to understand that your parent is tired and worried but still loves and needs you.

Having an Elderly Relative in Your Home. There may come a time when one of your grandparents is too old to live alone. He or she may need to come and live in your home where there will be people to look after him or her. This means that you may lose some of your privacy—perhaps even your own room.

When an elderly person comes to live in your home, your entire family will need to adjust. There will be another person at the table at mealtime, someone else with whom to share the television, and another person to give you orders!

It is not always easy to live with elderly people. Sometimes they are grumpy and complain about everything. They may be too cold or too warm. The music you play on your radio will be too loud. You will often be making too much noise. Sometimes they forget things or talk about things which you do not understand.

You may become angry and want to leave the room. It is natural for you to be upset. This person has changed the routine in your home. There is nothing you can do about it, however, because your parents feel responsible for this person and need to take care of them. Someday *you* may need to take *your* elderly parent into your home.

If the elderly person is able to talk about his or her life, you can take time to learn something from them. Grandparents and great aunts and uncles know a lot about your family history. Ask them to tell you what life was like when they were young. If they lived in the same town, have them tell you about how the buildings and streets have changed. Compare the subjects they studied in school with the ones that you are studying now. You may find that your relative is a great story-teller!

You may be able to learn a new skill or craft. If your elderly visitor can knit, crochet, carve wood, or play a musical instrument, ask him or her to teach you. If your family comes from a foreign background, your visitor may be able to teach you to cook some ethnic foods.

Give your elderly guest a chance to get to know you—even though you may be annoyed about him or her being there. They cannot get acquainted if you are always in your room. The elderly need to feel needed and they enjoy young people. They feel sad about growing old and not being able to do the things they could do when they were younger. Take time to get to know your guest. You may find that you have a new friend. Introduce your friends to your visitor. Help make them a part of your family.

There are books listed at the end of this chapter that will help you understand the aging process.

Handicaps. Not everyone is able to walk, see, speak, or hear as well as you and your friends. You may have a handicapped parent, brother, sister, friend, or classmate. They may be handicapped, but they are not necessarily disabled. Although people with handicaps may not be able to do some things, they still have feelings — just like you. They can laugh and joke, but they can also feel hurt, especially if people make fun of them. It is wrong to make fun of people who do not look or act the same as you.

A person with a handicap may be unable to do some things, but they may excel in other areas. A young person who cannot walk may be an expert at video games; a person who is hearing impaired may be a fine artist; a parent who is blind can still give love and support; a classmate who is in a wheelchair can still be a good friend; your handicapped brother or sister can still be a special companion on a rainy day.

The books at the end of this chapter will tell you more about what people with handicaps *can* do.

Moving Away. One of the scariest things that can happen to you is to have your family tell you that you are going to move. Your first reaction may be, "I'm not going... They can't make me go... I'll go and live with my friends... I'll run away." These are normal reactions, but none of them are very good ideas. You really have no control over the situation and you need to try and make the best of an unpleasant situation.

Your family may need to move because your parents are getting a divorce. Perhaps the parent with whom you will be living cannot afford to keep your current home. Your parents may be sad about the divorce and want to move away because he or she feels bad about living there without your other parent.

On the other hand, you may have to move because one or both of your parents has gotten a better job in another city or town. Parents have to think about having enough money both *today* and in the future. Sometimes they have to make these decisions that make you feel unhappy. It almost seems as though they don't care what you think, but they really do. It will be hard for them to say goodbye, too.

They know you will worry about a new school. "Will I know the material we have to study in the new school?... Does the school use the same books?... Will my teacher and I like each other?... Will there be kids in my new neighborhood?" Parents *do* understand, but they have to do what is best for all of you.

It will take a while for you to adjust to your new home and carve out a space for yourself. It may be difficult to make new friends at first. Remember, the kids in your new school may be shy about a new person. They may not come running to you. You may have to meet them half way by introducing yourself or inviting someone to your home. Stay with your group on the playground instead of going off by yourself. If you are good at a sport or other activity, let the others know. Do not try to impress the new kids with what you have. Show them yourself, not a phony. Talk to your seatmate on the bus. Start a conversation about his or her notebook or an article of clothing. Ask your new classmates about projects they are doing or for directions around the school. Ask about clubs and sports.

Everyone else will know the routines. This will be hard for you. Sometimes it is difficult to ask questions. You are sure you'll sound dumb and everyone will laugh. The new kids may test you just to see if you are a good sport. Try not to get mad. If you show that you *are* a good sport, you will have many new friends real soon.

You do not have to forget about your old friends just because you have had to move to another neighborhood. Old friendships can continue and can help the making of new friends be a little easier. If your parents will allow it, make a telephone call to one of your old friends. Use a kitchen timer so you will not talk too long. Write letters back and forth. Make a tape telling your old friends what you are doing in your new school and your new neighborhood. Tell them about your new town. Perhaps you can plan to have them come and visit on a weekend or during school vacation.

Your parents may *not* always know what you are thinking and feeling about the move unless you tell them. Remember that they are trying to adjust to a new place, too. They may forget about your worries. Talk to them. You both may be surprised to find out that you are having similar feelings about being in your new home.

Books for You To Read

TROUBLE AT HOME
Gilbert, Sasa. *Trouble At Home,* New York: Lothrop, Lee and Shepard Books, 1981.

ALCOHOL ABUSE
Englebardt, Stanley L. *Kids and Alcohol,* New York: Lothrop, Lee and Shepard Company, 1975.

Evans, Roberta. *Alcohol and Alcoholism,* New York: Franklin Watts Publishing Company, 1976.

Lee, Essie and Israel, Elaine. *Alcohol and You,* New York: Julian Messner, 1975.

North, Robert and Orange, Richard Jr. *Teen Age Drinking: The #1 Drug Threat to Young People Today,* New York: Collier Books, 1981.

Seixas, Judith S. *Living With A Parent Who Drinks Too Much,* New York: Greenwillow Books, 1979.

DEATH
Anderson, Lydia. *Death,* New York: Franklin Watts, Inc., 1980.

Grollman, Earl A. *Talking About Death*, Boston: Beacon Press, 1976.

McHugh, Mary. *Young People Talk About Death*, New York: Franklin Watts, Inc. 1980.

Steinberg, Franki and Steinberg, Barbara. *Exploring Death with Young People*, Englewood Cliffs, New Jersey: Prentice-Hall Inc., 1980.

Rofes, Eric E. *The Kids' Book About Death and Dying,* Boston: Little-Brown Publishing Company, to be published in 1985.

ABOUT ILL SIBLINGS
Murray, Gloria and Jampolsky, Gerald G., Eds. *Straight From the Siblings: Another Look at the Rainbow,* Millbrae, California: Celestial Arts, 1982.

HANDICAPS

Adams, Barbara. *Like It Is: Facts And Feelings About Handicaps From Kids Who Know,* New York: Walker and Company, 1979.

Kamien, Janet. *What If You Couldn't?...* New York: Charles Scribner's Sons, 1979.

Smith, Lucia B. *A Special Kind of Sister,* New York: Holt, Rinehart and Winston, 1979.

Sullivan, Mary Beth, Brightman, Alan B., and Blatt, Joseph. *Feeling Free,* Reading, Massachusetts: Addison-Wesley, 1979.

Thomas, William E. *The New Boy Is Blind,* New York: Julian Messner, 1980.

Wolf, Bernard. *Connie's New Eyes,* New York: J. B. Lippincot Co., 1976.

UNDERSTANDING THE ELDERLY

Ancona, George. *Growing Older,* New York: E. P. Dutton and Co., Inc., 1978.

Farber, Norma. *How Does It Feel To Be Old?* New York: E. P. Dutton and Co., Inc., 1979.

Shanks, Ann Zane. *Old Is What You Get: Dialogues On Aging By The Old and The Young,* New York: The Viking Press, 1976.

Sobol, Harriet Langsam. *Grandpa—A Young Man Grown Old,* New York: Coward, McCann and Geoghagan, Inc., 1980.

5.

Going to a Specialty Camp

If you are too young to work, how about going to camp? Camp isn't merely for little kids. There are many specialty camps available which are geared to the interests of young people. Check your school district, the "Y" or any other youth organizations in your community. Many have computer camps where you can learn about operating a computer. Other camps feature sports—basketball, swimming, baseball and tennis. If you are interested in the arts, you may find a music, art or drama camp in your area.

Many of these camps are inexpensive. Perhaps you can split the cost with your parents by saving some of your allowance and putting it toward your camp fee.

Some camps offer counselor-in-training programs where you spend a summer learning to be a paid counselor for the following season. If you enjoy working with children, you can get some experience here. Camp may be the beginning of career planning for your future. So, put your summer to good use. Learn a new skill or improve on an old one.

Your parents may be interested in sending you to overnight camp. If you have never been away before, the idea may be rather scary for you. Being on your own in a supervised place, however, is one of the first steps to being grown up. But being away can cause mixed feelings. You want to be grown up, but you are afraid to let go. It's o.k. to feel scared about going away, even though some of your friends are going, too.

Work it out with your family to call home if you need to. Get to know your counselor, who will always be ready to talk if you need some extra company. Be ready to participate in all camp activities. Other young people like yourself may be nervous about being away from home. Get involved! Remember, a camping experience will give you a feeling of independence and help you get ready for other separations such as going to college.

Use the following list to help choose the right camp for you.

TEN TIPS TO HELP YOU AND YOUR FAMILY CHOOSE A CAMP

1. Does the camp feature computers, sports, drama or other areas of special interest to you?
2. What kinds of activities will you do during the day?
3. Will you be with people your age?
4. Will there be both boys and girls in the camp?
5. Will you be able to call or write home?
6. Will you be allowed visitors?
7. Where will you be sleeping?
8. What type of swimming facilities are available?
9. Will you be near any of your friends?
10. What time is "lights out?"

6.

Failing Does Not Mean You Are a Failure

Every young person has to go to school until a certain age, depending on the state law. Sometimes you won't like going to school. One year you may have a teacher that you like and then have one that you can't stand the following year. You may even think that he or she doesn't like kids. It may look that way. Teachers are individuals, just like everyone else. Some are very friendly and concerned. Others are quite strict and seem to be all business and no fun. Just because a teacher is strict, however, doesn't mean that he or she does not understand what young people are thinking.

Both you and your teachers have important jobs. They must teach and you must learn. Neither they nor you can do the job alone. With cooperation and understanding, the jobs can be completed, making both you and your teacher pleased.

Occasionally, things do not go well in school and you may find yourself failing a subject. This may happen because you have not tried very hard. Often it is difficult to do your best if you don't like the subject or the teacher. There may be times when you don't understand the work but are afraid to ask questions. You may feel that your friends will think you are dumb. You are not being fair to yourself when you let this happen. Good marks are important later when you want to go to college or get a job, but that may not be easy for you to understand right now.

Your parents may come down hard on you for not doing well in school. They may want you to have the opportunities they did not have when they were young. They may want you to do better in school than they did. Sometimes they will compare you with a brother, sister, or friend who always does well in school. They forget that young people are all different from each other. Try to sit down and talk to your folks. Remind them in a quiet way that *you* are *you* and that some school subjects are harder for one person than another.

In some cases, it may seem as though your parents do not care if you are not doing well in school. It may look that way because they do not know what to say or do. If parents did not do well in school or had bad experiences with teachers when they were young, they may feel uneasy about trying to help you. They may not feel comfortable talking to your teachers. It doesn't mean that they don't care, it only means that they don't know what to say. Then *you* have to take the responsibility for solving your own problem.

Many young people get into difficulty at school because they do not do their homework. Homework *does* take time away from other things you enjoy such as playing with your friends and watching television. Homework is, however, just what it says —*work* to do at *home.* Teachers assign this to give you extra practice with the skill you are learning *and* to give you responsibility for doing some work on your own. Even though you may think so, teachers do *not* give you homework to keep you from doing the things you like to do! When you don't do your homework, teachers get annoyed. Don't bother giving them excuses like "the dog ate it." They have heard them all!

If you have trouble keeping track of the homework you are asked to do, get yourself a small pad to keep in your notebook or pocket. Write down your assignments and when they are due. Many grown-ups need to write down what they have to do every day. Get yourself into the habit of knowing what is expected of you every day.

Failing Does Not Mean You Are a Failure

You may need some help getting yourself organized for school every day—like carpenters making sure they have the correct tools for the job. You cannot do your work accurately if you leave your books and pens at home. Your work may be affected if you forget your lunch and don't eat. It is hard to pay attention when your empty stomach is growling with hunger! Some people are good at remembering things while others are not. If you forget your school equipment, and your parents are working and cannot bring things to you, you are out of luck for that day. When you were in the primary grades, teachers kept reminding you about the materials you needed. Now your classes are larger, you are older, and you are expected to look after yourself. Keeping track of your own school supplies is another way that you can assume responsibility in a grown-up world. Keep a checklist for yourself at home to remind you of what you need to bring with you to school each day. A sample list is included at the end of this chapter.

When things are not going well in school, it is important to find out why they aren't, and what you can do about it. Try to talk to your teacher. Make an appointment to see him or her. You may need extra help after school either by yourself or with other students. Even though you would rather be out with your friends, it is important to do what you can for yourself to improve your marks.

Your teacher may suggest that you have a tutor—another teacher or person who can give you extra help with the troublesome subject. A tutor can be a big help because he or she may be able to explain things in a different way than your teacher and you may better understand the work.

With some young people, no matter how hard they try, nothing works and they fail the subject. Don't give up. It is easy to say "I'm dumb anyway," or "I don't care." Everyone is good in one thing, at least. Some are good at reading, some in art or music. You, too, will have some special area but you will need to find out exactly what it is.

There are ways to find help.

Most schools have people called counselors or psychologists who work with teachers to find out why students fail and what their strengths may be. You may have to spend some time talking with them and taking some simple tests. You can help yourself by answering their questions honestly and telling the counselor about the things that may be bothering you about school or your classes.

Sometimes you really don't know what is happening to you. You are confused and things are not working right. Occasionally, a small problem makes everything else go wrong. Just like a car, if the engine isn't working correctly, the car won't go. If you feel bad about yourself — either about schoolwork or about family problems — nothing else will go right either. There is nothing to be ashamed of if you ask for help. If you broke your arm, you would have to go to the doctor to have it fixed. If something is bothering you inside, you have to tell someone about it so it can be fixed.

Troubles at home may affect the work that you do in school. It is hard to think about classes and homework when you are worried about something that is happening with your family. The way you feel about school can be seriously affected if your parents are getting a divorce, if someone loses his or her job, or if a member of your family is seriously ill. It would help you to tell your teacher or counselor what is happening. Teachers are trained to know what to say and what to do for young people who are experiencing problems at home. They will understand if you are having a bad day because you are upset or angry. Your parents may not want you to say anything to anybody about what goes on at home. They may feel unsure and embarrassed. It is important, however, that you do all that you can to help yourself do the best job that you can in school. Having understanding teachers may be your key to success. They cannot help, however, if they don't know what is troubling you.

You may feel that you cannot talk about your problems with anyone at school or at home. Don't be afraid to look for help on your own. Do you belong to a church or temple group, the "Y," the boys' or girls' club, scouts or other youth group? If you feel comfortable with the leader, tell him or her what you are feeling about school. Talking things out can make you feel better about what you need to do and whom you need to see.

Talking to a friend's mom or dad may be easy for you. There are times when you feel that other people's parents can give better advice and understand more than your own. This is because it is often easier to talk to people that are not part of your own family.

The important thing to remember is to talk — talk to your teachers, counselors, parents, or leaders. They will have important advice that will help you to get back on the right track with your school work.

GETTING READY FOR SCHOOL CHECK-LIST

Use this list as a sample and add the items you need to get yourself ready for school each day.

Writing implements (pens, pencils, ruler)
Books
Homework
Lunch
Snack
Gym clothing
Musical instrument
Notes from home
Key
Rain gear

7.

Surviving Peer Pressure

Friends are very important people. Everyone *needs* friends and wants to be liked by them. Most of the time you want to do the same things they do, say the things they say, and wear the same clothes they wear. Young people are highly influenced by their friends. We call this influence "peer pressure." Peer is another word for a friend or a classmate who is your age.

Because young people need to be accepted and liked by their friends, they want to look like them, either by wearing the same hair style or the same type of clothing. When everyone wears the same kinds of clothing, we call this a "fad." Many fads die out quickly. Others last a longer time. You know how important it is to have athletic shoes like the ones your friends have or wear shirts with alligators on them or jeans with a special designer's name on the back pocket.

When young people try to keep up with what others are wearing, they often get into trouble with their parents. This happens because clothes that are "in style" are often very expensive. Parents do not like to pay lots of money for young people's clothes—especially while they are still growing. At your age, your feet could be one size in March and a size larger in September. Your forty dollar name-brand athletic shoes may not fit and you will have had them only six months.

Another reason some parents do not like to see everyone dressing alike is because of something called "individuality." Individuality means being yourself — an individual — doing what *you* feel is right and doing what *you* want to do. Many parents would like to see their children be individuals and not always be like one of the group. Sometimes you should be an engine and lead rather than a caboose that always follows. Start your own fad!

Your parents may be more willing to let you have expensive name-brand clothing if you agree to pay half of the cost yourself. You should not *expect* them to buy these for you just because they are your parents and are supposed to buy your clothes. You will have to decide if wearing all the latest style clothing is worth spending some of your own money.

Peer pressure can lead to competition — trying to be the best at something or better than somebody else. Remember when you were in the primary grades and other children pushed to be the *first* in line? Remember when somebody in the class bragged about being the *best* reader or the *fastest* runner? Sometimes it was difficult to like those people and you probably thought they were bossy or show-offs.

Many times competition shows up in sports. For many young people, being active in sports is important. Their parents encourage them to participate in baseball, football, soccer, swimming, gymnastics, and other team sports. There will always be someone who is the top player — number one. *You* may not be the top player no matter how hard you try. You may not even *like* playing sports but feel that you have to do it because your friends do.

Many sports depend on the size of your body for success. You do not have any control over how fast your body develops. If you are still short or thin for your age, you may not be the best player or team member.

It is silly to spend a lot of time and money for equipment on something you do not like. You may not be good at sports but there

Surviving Peer Pressure

will be something else at which you will do well.

Remember, not everybody can be number one. It may be discouraging and even painful to keep trying. If you still like the sport, then accept the fact that you may be number two or even number three. It is not that important to be the star. The star of the team cannot shine without the help of the other players and that includes *you*.

In some cases, peer pressure can be dangerous. Have you ever had anyone say to you "I bet you can't do it . . . Are you chicken? . . . Come on, nobody will ever know." Chances are, a friend may have said these words to you when he or she was trying to get you to do something that was not right. There are times when friends can get you into serious trouble when you are off playing. Vandalism — destroying property that belongs to other people — often happens when one young person dares another to do something. Destroying the property of others is a crime and getting caught will mean getting involved with the police. You may not get caught, but that does not make what you did right. You were lucky that one time. You may, however, be the one who gets caught while the friends who had the idea stand back or run away and say nothing.

Young people often become involved with shoplifting — taking things from stores without paying for them. It looks easy and a friend may tell you that it is a way of getting a toy or an article of clothing that you have always wanted. Shoplifting, however, is *stealing* and the police must be called for people who steal. Even if you do not get caught the first time, you probably will if you try again. The store officials will call your parents and maybe even the police.

If any of your friends ask you to trade or sell any of your belongings, make sure that you ask your parents first. Do not take an item from a friend's home even though he or she tells you that it is o.k. When your parents buy clothes and toys for you, they expect you to keep them. Although it may be fun to trade things and have new clothes and toys, it is best to check with your parents first.

Taking money from your parent's wallet or purse may be a temptation. Your friends may do it and tell you to do it. They may tell you that your parents will never know. This is *stealing,* even though it is from your parents. If they *do* find out, they will not trust you any more and you may have to spend a great deal of time rebuilding that trust. If you need money, talk to your parents about increasing your allowance or about ways that you can earn some extra money.

Some young people may ask you for money in return for "protection." Someone may say, "If you give me a dollar every week, I'll make sure nobody beats you up, takes your lunch, or teases you on the bus." This is against the law. If a grown-up did this, the police would call it "extortion" and the person asking for the money would be arrested. If this happens to you, don't pay anybody any money. Tell your parents or your teacher right away.

Deep down inside you know if what you are doing is against the law or against what your parents would like you to do. If your friends are trying to talk you into something you know is wrong, put the blame on your family. Tell them "my mom or dad would really be mad." Or, if you feel something is wrong, tell your friends, "I think it is a dumb idea," and walk away. When the little voice inside you is telling you that something is a bad idea, listen to it carefully. You will be a stronger person for having been a good listener to that voice. If you are unsure about what some of your friends are doing, try to talk with an adult—parent, teacher, friend's parent, or youth group leader. They can give you some good advice about listening to yourself.

If you *do* get caught doing something against the rules, you will have to accept the consequences of what you did. You may have to go to the police station to wait for your parents to come and get you. This is embarrassing. The police will tell you that what you did was wrong and that a more serious punishment may be in store for you next time.

You may be asked to make restitution for the damage you did. This means you will have to work to pay for it or work to clean it up. If you have to spend a few Saturdays cleaning paint from a wall, you may think twice about doing the damage next time.

Many times these troubles occur because you and your friends have nothing to do. This is why it is a good idea for all of you to be involved in a recreational after-school or vacation program in your school, the "Y," church or temple, or other community group.

Drug abuse is something you hear about often these days. There are several reasons why young people use drugs: to escape from problems at school, in the family, or with friends; curiosity, wanting to know what drugs are all about; and peer pressure, because your friends talk you into it. None of these are good reasons for using drugs. Drugs like pills and marijuana will make you feel happy, but not for long. When the effects wear off, you still have to face yourself and others. The problems will still be there.

Drugs are dangerous. They can make you seriously ill. In some cases, you may never get better. They can have an effect on your school work. Eventually, you will not be able to keep your mind on what you are doing, and your grades will be poor. Your personality will change. Instead of being a happy person, you will become moody and depressed. You may lose your friends and get into trouble with your family.

People can become addicted to drugs. This means that they cannot stop taking them, even if they want to. Drugs then become a bad habit. Drugs are also expensive. You cannot afford to buy them on the allowance your family gives you. Most young people are unable to afford a drug habit. When they run out of money, they steal things and sell them for money to buy drugs. If they are caught, they are arrested.

Drugs are illegal. Even marijuana or pot is illegal. When you do something illegal, the law becomes involved. Your parents will be called and a judge will probably send you to a drug treatment center where you will receive help to kick the drug habit. Even if you are *not* addicted yet, you will have to pay a penalty for having been caught using drugs. This is not a happy way to begin your life.

Remember, if a friend offers you marijuana or some pills to make you feel "good," refuse them. It is wrong to abuse your body with substances that can become habit forming like drugs, alcohol, and tobacco. Sadly enough, many adults have these habits, but that does not make them grown-up things to do.

You may consider smoking cigarettes and drinking beer or other alcohol to be a grown-up activity. Many adults have become seriously ill because of the effects of alcohol and smoking.

If you begin to drink at an early age, you could become an alcoholic. There *are* twelve year old alcoholics who cannot stop drinking. Unless they seek help through a group called Alcoholics Anonymous, their lives will be destroyed before they are in their late teens.

The label on a pack of cigarettes says, ". . . smoking may be hazardous to your health." This label was placed there to let you know that doctors really believe that smoking causes lung cancer, heart disease, and other respiratory problems. If you become addicted to smoking cigarettes now while you are young, you may not escape these illnesses later on. If you do not smoke, don't start. If you *do* smoke, please stop before cigarettes take control of you.

Parents may become upset when they do not approve of their children's friends. This is a natural concern because parents *were* kids once and they know the kinds of trouble young people can get into when they are encouraged by their friends.

If your parents know that one of your friends does not have a good reputation, they will not want you to spend time with that person. They are afraid that you will be influenced and perhaps get into trouble yourself.

Parents really worry when you pal around with friends who drive. Young people can be careless drivers when the car is filled with happy friends. They may drive too fast or be careless in bad weather conditions. Your parents would never want to get a call from the police telling them that you had been injured or killed in an automobile accident.

It is difficult for you to give up friends because your parents do not approve. Most young people argue with their folks and continue to see their friends secretly. This is a bad idea because you are ruining any trust that may have developed between you and your parents. If you truly feel that your parents are being unfair in their opinion of your friends, bring them to your home so that your parents can get to know them. Maybe your friends *can* be trusted and maybe your parents were wrong. Sometimes it is difficult for parents to let you grow up and make your own decisions. Talk things out so you will understand exactly what your folks expect of you and your friends.

You may as well forget the old argument that starts with "Everyone else is doing it," or "All the other kids' parents let them." This does not work. Your parents will tell you that you are not "everybody" and they care about what is good for *you*. One parent actually decided to telephone her child's friend's parents to see if "all the other kids' parents" really were letting them go to a party that had no adult supervision. She found out that the other parents did not know the party was unchaperoned. Consequently, nobody went to the party.

In some cases, other parents do let their children do things that your parents will not let you do. They may feel that the activity is not right for *you* at this time. They need to trust their better judgment. It will make you angry and your home life may be quite unpleasant for a while. Your parents, however, are usually right. Remember, they have had many more years of experience interacting with people than you have had. They know from reading and observing other young people what kinds of trouble can occur. They still love you *and* trust you, but need to protect you until you have had more years of experience.

GROWING UP IS...

Many families argue about curfews—how late you are allowed to stay out at night. Your parents should always know where you are if you need to be out after dark. If they tell you to be home at eight o'clock, they *mean* eight o'clock and not eight fifteen. Wear a watch so you will not have the excuse "I didn't know what time it was." Parents may accept that excuse once, but the next time you may be grounded. Having to stay at home while all your friends are playing or going to the movies is not a happy experience.

You should never be out after dark unless there is a special event. If you have to walk home, walk with friends. If you stop someplace, call your parents to tell them where you are. Always carry enough money for a phone call. If you are on your way home and someone or something frightens you, run quickly and try to get to a telephone.

If your parents insist on a curfew, it is because they worry about accidents and other problems that can occur when young people are on their own away from home. Avoid standing around on street corners and other hangouts. Go to school sponsored or community sponsored events. Visit your friends at their homes. Take turns visiting each other on weekend evenings.

If you feel that your curfew is unreasonable, try and negotiate a new one with your folks. They may bend the rules if you can give them good reasons for your request. If your new curfew is denied, it will probably be because they do not feel that it is wise for you to be away from your home so late in the evening.

Nobody ever said that growing up would be easy. It is important to be liked by your friends, but it is *just* as important to know right from wrong and *not* to take dares. Remember that it is o.k. to be "chicken." "Chickens" do not get into trouble with their parents, teachers, or the police.

8.

Conclusion

Now that you have read *Growing Up Is...*, you should have a better idea of some of the problems you and your friends may have as you are growing up. All young people have problems—some more than others. Your problems and concerns may have to do with your family, your friends or your school. At times, you may even have difficulties with all three!

When things are bothering you, you need to talk about them. The most important people with whom you should talk are your parents. Your parents are not mind readers, however. *You* may need to take the lead in trying to talk because they may be unsure of how to talk with young people. If this happens, nobody speaks to anybody and the bad feelings keep building up inside of everyone involved. Treat your parents as you would want them to treat you. Sometimes just a hug can make them feel good and open the doors to communication.

If you feel that you cannot talk to your parents, find someone else whom you can trust. Adults are good people with whom to talk because they have had many more years of experience with life than you have had. Even if they cannot directly help you, they can be good listeners.

Remember that you are an important person. There will be times when nothing seems to go right. You must not give up on yourself. It is o.k. to be angry, scared or upset. Try to solve your problems as best as you can. Talk to your friends. You will find out that you are not alone. Many of the same things bother and confuse them.

If your friends are having difficulties, remember that they need help from someone with whom they can talk. Be a good listener for them and give them the support that they need. There may be times when you will want them to listen to you.

Growing up has never been easy for anyone. Sometimes it will seem really difficult for you. Most everyone seems to get through their younger years. You will do it too.

APPENDIX 1

What Would You Do?

The following situations might happen to you when you are on your own. What will you do? Whom will you call? Read and discuss them with a friend or your parent(s).

1. You and your younger sister are home by yourselves after school. You open your closet door and see smoke. What will you do? What if you lived in an apartment building?

2. As you are on your way home from school one day, a woman in a car stops beside you, calls you by name, and tells you that your mother sent her to pick you up. What will you do?

3. A friend you've wanted to play with for a long time wants you to come to his home after school. You really want to go but your mom is expecting you to call when you get home. What will you say or do?

4. As you are opening a can of food to feed the cat, you cut your hand on the can. The cut is bleeding. What will you do?

5. You and your friend are in the store. Your friend tells you that it's o.k. to put a toy car in your pocket and not pay for it. He says nobody will see you. What will you do?

6. The telephone rings when you are home alone after school. A man asks if your mom is home. What will you say?

7. While you are home alone after school, two people you do not know come to the door and ring the bell. What will you say?

8. Although your parents have told you never to have friends in the house when there are no adults at home, two of your young neighbors want to come in to play. They tell you that your parents will never know. What will you say?

APPENDIX 2

Organizations for Young People

Look in your telephone book for the telephone numbers of these organizations in your community.

Big Brother Association
Big Sister Association
Young Men's Christian/Hebrew Association
Young Women's Christian/Hebrew Association
Boy Scouts of America
Girl Scouts of America
Boys' Club of America
Girls' Club of America
Camp Fire Girls
Alcoholics Anonymous or Alateen

Other Groups that Deal with Alcoholism

The National Association for Children of Alcoholics (NACOA) P.O. Box 421691, San Francisco, California 94142; 415-431-1366

The Children of Alcoholics Foundation, 540 Madison Avenue, New York, New York 10022; 212-980-5394

Index

A

Accidents
    prevention, 41-42, 47-48
    rules to prevent, 48
After-school programs, 48
Alcohol abuse
    adults, 55
    Alateen, 56, 59
    young people, 86

C

Camp
    choosing, 70
    specialty camp, 69
Child abuse, 60
Competition, 78-80
Counselors
    guidance, 76
Curfew, 88

D

Death
    of family member, 61
Dial-a-Pal, 48-49
Divorce, 19, 23-24
Drug abuse
    adults, 59
    young people, 84-85

E

Elderly relatives, 61-63
Emergencies
    accident, 46-47
    checklist, 47
    fire, 45

F

Failure in school, 71
Families
    divorced, 23-24
    single parent, 24
    stepfamilies, 24-26
Family problems, 53
Fire
    drills, 45
    escape route, 45
    hazards in home, 45
    in home, 45
    on clothing, 45
    on stove, 45
Fireplace, 46

H

Handicaps, 64
Homework, 72
House rules
    check list, 49
    need, 39

I

Illness
    alone at home, 42
    parents, 62
    siblings, 62
    taking medicine, 43

K

Keys
    losing, 39
    wearing, 39
Kidnapping, 40

Index

L
Listening, 17, 34, 90

M
Meals
   clean-up, 41
   preparation, 41-42
Money
   budget sample, 36
   earning your own, 35-36
Moving, 64-66

O
Organizations, 93

P
Peer pressure
   clothing, 79
   competition, 79-80
   drugs, 84-85
   friends, 79, 85-86
   protection money, 84
   shoplifting, 83
   stealing from parents, 84
Pipes leaking, 47
Power outage, 47

S
School
   at home before, 45
   check list, 77
   failure, 76
Sick
   being at home, 42
   taking medicine, 43
Single parents, 24

Smoking
   cigarettes, 86
   marijuana, 84-85
Snacks
   preparing, 41
   safety, 41
   snack ideas, 50
Social worker, 60
Stepfamilies, 24-26
Strangers
   at the door, 46
   claiming to be "friend," 47
   in cars, 47
   in the hallway, 46-47
   on the telephone, 46

T
Telephone
   messages, 40
   number list, 51
   parents at work, 39-40
   strangers who call, 46
Tutor, 75

U
Unemployment, 53

V
Vandalism, 83

W
Working families, 29

Y
Younger children
   caring for, 42